STORY TELLING
NEW
&
OLD

by
Padraic Colum

decorations by
Jay Van Everen

THE MACMILLAN COMPANY
New York

This essay first appeared in Padraic Colum's book
The Fountain of Youth, Copyright 1927 by
The Macmillan Company. All rights reserved.

The Macmillan Company, New York
Collier-Macmillan Canada, Ltd., Toronto, Ontario
Library of Congress catalog card number: 68-13553
Printed in the United States of America
Reissued February, 1968
FIRST PRINTING

"IMAGINATION IS THE BEGINNING
OF CREATION.
YOU IMAGINE WHAT YOU DESIRE;
YOU WILL WHAT YOU IMAGINE;
AND AT LAST YOU CREATE WHAT YOU WILL."

STORY TELLING, NEW AND OLD

It has been discovered that there is still a place in the world for an oral art—for story-telling. Those who have charge of children's reading rooms in American libraries have had to rediscover and exercise that art, for children who come to borrow books remain to have stories told them. And so we have the most ancient of the arts being carried on in modern surroundings. At the suggestion of some of those modern and metropolitan story-tellers, the librarians, this book has been put together: the stories in it have been reshaped from stories in other books, and they have been put into such forms and such words as make it possible to deliver them naturally and simply by the human voice.

The story-teller whom I listened to when I was young had many advantages over the story-teller in one of our public libraries. He told his stories in the evening; he told them by the light of a candle and a peat fire—often by the light of a peat fire only. There were shadows upon the walls around. Nothing that he told us had to be visualized in the glare of day or by the glare of electric light. He had a language that had not been written down; he had words that had not been made colorless by constant use in books and newspapers. He was free to make all sorts of rhymes and chimes in the language he used, and to use words that were meaningless except for the overtones of meaning that were in their sounds. He had various tags with which to end his stories. And he

could make his hero start from the hilltop that was known to all his audience, and he could have his battle fought upon the strand that they had all been upon. His audience was small, no more than a score of people, and so he could be intimate in voice and manner. He had few gestures, this particular story-teller: sometimes he beat his hands together; sometimes he raised a stick that was by him to give solemnity to some happening. And outside was the silence of the night and the silence of a countryside.

All this is to say that the story-teller of my childhood days had a convention—a convention that he was master of and that was looked for and accepted by his audience. From him I learned that a story that is to be told has to be about happenings. That it has to be in sentences that can be easily and pleasantly carried over by the human voice. That it has nothing to say about states of mind. That in its descriptions it has to be free of generalities—not a catalogue of a poet's association with the sea by way of description, let us say, but the flash of the wave. That its characters should be explicable at every moment, even though they do odd and unpredictable things. And that they must be the kind of human beings that the human voice can shepherd—and the voice cannot shepherd divided, many-mooded, complicated people.

It would be well if the modern and metropolitan story-teller could do what that story-teller's art permitted him to do—to make certain descriptions purely conventional—the description of a ship sailing the sea, for instance; the description of a castle or of a lonely waste. By such con-

ventionalizations he was able to get what every one who undertakes to tell a story of some length has to try to get, points of rest, passages that are relief in the narrative. When he set his ship sailing upon the sea, when he set this hero wandering through a wilderness, the audience rested and the story-teller rested, not because there was nothing happening, but because what was happening was regular and anticipated. These conventionalized descriptions ("runs" the story-teller called them) were so placed in the story that they gave rests where rests were needed; they gave relief in the method of delivery, too, for the "run" was always spoken with a quicker rhythm, as if it were a piece of free verse; sometimes it was spoken to the beating of the story-teller's hands. "He set off, and there was blackening on his soles, and holing in his shoes; the little birds were taking their rests at the butts of bushes and the tops of the trees, but if they were, he was not." How often has a "run" like this, and "runs" that were longer, occurred in the recital of a story of some quest. And such "runs," woven into it at intervals, give a more definite pattern to a story.

In the story told by the professional story-teller, or by that amateur of story-telling, the nurse in old countries, there

are certain possessions of the hero or hero-
ine—a sword, a helmet, a dress, a comb
—that have to be made memorable. The
story-teller shows his delights in such possessions; he makes them, not so much possessions as attributes of his hero or hero-
ine: the mention of them recalls or fore-
shadows a happening. To be able to use
such a possession in a story is to be able
to give another gleam, to give another in-
terest to it.

7

They have reverie behind them, these stories that have such patterns, such series of happenings, such simplicity of characterization as make it possible to deliver them orally to an unselected audience. This is true of traditional stories, and true of the stories for children that writers such as Hans Andersen and Rudyard Kipling have made up. And the best story-tellers are the men and women who seem to be giving us in the stories they are telling fragments of their reverie: no matter how exciting the incidents they relate there is always reverie behind them. It is this quality of reverie, this dramatizing of something different from what is in our external consciousness, that makes the story told distinct from the story that is written to be read by the reader. It seems to me that a story that can be told has a value distinct from the value that belongs to a story that is for the reader—it carries over feelings that belong to something deeper in us than our external consciousness. And the art of the story-teller, I think, consists in giving spontaneity to a series of happenings. They have to be in formal series, for the story has to have distinct pattern. But the story-teller has to relate the happenings as if he or she had just discovered them as something going on. The pattern of the story has to be a familiar one, the characters in it have to have such simplicity that they can be presented directly and understood immediately.

Poetry As Well

One has to talk of poetry, in so far as it is oral, in connection with oral stories. Children should be got not merely to read and know poetry, but to possess some part of the heritage of poetry. They should know poems by heart—a dozen, twenty, forty, fifty poems. These poems should be there so that at any time they might well up within their minds. Plato put music amongst the subjects it was important to have youth trained in. Nowadays we do not look upon music as Plato looked upon it, as a foundation for knowledge; to us music is a separate course of study. And yet, when we think of what poetry, with its rhythm and structure, can give to childhood, we begin to feel that we understand why Plato put music with the few fundamental things that youth should have a training in.

We know that both poetry and music have something underlying them that holds our attention, that helps us to bring our minds to a focus. That underlying something is rhythm. The holding in the mind of certain rhythms—the rhythms of certain tunes, the rhythms of certain poems —gives us foundations for building on in our imaginative and intellectual life. A poem is a piece of human speech that can be mastered, whole or in passages, and kept in the memory. Its rhythm, its rhymes, are holds that we have on it. And when we have it in our memory we have something that our thoughts can focus themselves on. The person who has a dozen or so of poems in his or her memory has charms against straying thoughts. If he or she knows by heart an ode by Keats or by Shelley, his thoughts or her thoughts can be held by rhythm, by structure, and they will not be hopelessly scattered. And by holding our thoughts from being scattered we win a victory for the mind.

The poems we hold in our minds are points of focus, patterns of order. Perhaps it was to give such points, such patterns, that Plato advocated a training in music as a foundation for general knowledge. Of course, there are other means than by poetry or music to get points of focus, patterns of order, into our minds. A technical or professional training that would ignore music and poetry could, no doubt, supply them. But the patterns of order left by poetry or by music are imaginative, and, therefore, are creative. Our minds become aroused by going over them; in a poem the rhythm, the rhymes, the images, suggest other rhythms, rhymes, and images. More than this: the great thing that a poem gives us when we refer to it in memory is a sense of something begun and finished—a thing complete.

Stories Again

"I am persuaded that both children and the lower class of readers hate books which are written down to their capacity," Walter Scott noted on one occasion. "They love those that are composed for their elders and betters. I will make, if possible, a book that a child will understand, yet a man will feel some temptation to peruse should he chance to take it up . . . the grand and interesting consists in ideas, not words." Scott, surely, was right in what he noted in these sentences. The story-teller must have respect for the child's mind and the child's conception of the world, knowing it for a complete mind and a complete conception. If a story-teller have that respect he need not be childish in his language in telling stories to children. If the action be clear and the sentences clear one can use a mature language. Strange words, out-of-the-way words do not bewilder children if there be order in the action and in the sentences.

They like to hear such words. Children love language for its own sake; they treasure words as they treasure keepsakes. It is worth while to note that in American schools, where children are used only to a standardized language, they are particularly attracted to poetry in dialect.

It is more important to let a child's imagination develop than it is to labor to inculcate in him or her some correct ethical point of view. If a child have in his or her mind the images that imaginative literature can communicate—the heroic, sweet, or loving types that are in the world's great stories—it is much more likely that he or she will grow up into a fine human being than if some austere mentor spoke to them out of every page of their reading. I think the mood of a story that is to be told to children should be one of kindliness. I do not mean that the characters in a story should be always kind to each other. I mean that those in the audience should be assured that the teller is inspired with a mood of kindliness for his conspicuous character. "Now you must know that the King had no horse to give Boots but an old broken-down jade," says the Norse story, "for his six other sons had carried off all the horses; but Boots did not care a pin for that; he sprang up on his sorry old steed. 'Farewell, father,' said he, 'I'll come back, never fear, and like enough I shall bring my brothers with me'; and with that he rode off." When we in the audience hear this we know that the teller of the tale has the right feeling for his hero.

With the mood of kindliness there should be the mood of adventure. The hero should be one who is willing to take strange paths in the morning and lie down under the giant's roof when the darkness falls. "After that they went around the castle, and at last they came to a great hall where the Trolls' two great swords hung high up on the wall. 'I wonder if you are man enough to wield one of these,' said the Princess. 'Who? I?' said the lad, ' 'twould be a pretty thing indeed if I couldn't wield one of these.' With that he put two or three chairs atop of the other, jumped up, and touched the biggest sword with his finger tips, tossed it up in the air, and caught it again by the hilt; leaped down, and, at the same time, dealt such a blow with it on the floor that the whole hall shook." That is the humor proper to a hero. The good characters in the story should undoubtedly be fine and upright, but we should not insist on their being always good boys at school. If they are heroic and adventurous and have a simple-minded goodness it is enough; the stories they figure in need not bristle with moralities and recommendations to good conduct. And the old figures of romance should be left to the children. When Kings, Queens, and Princes have taken their leave of the political world they should still be left to flourish in the world of the child's romance. Witches, giants, dwarfs, gnomes, and trolls should be left to them, too.

Things need not be too simplified in

that world. It will do no harm if things are left mysterious there—such mysterious things are "magic," and "magic" is an element that is not only accepted but is looked for. The probabilities that we know of from experience have no place in the world of the story that is primarily intended for a child. A tree may talk, a swan may change into a king's daughter, a castle may be built up in an instant. We know tree, swan, and castle by their limitations; but a child knows them in their boundless possibilities. To a child each thing that is mentioned is distinct, unique, a thing in itself, having all the possibilities of a thing in Eden. Did we not know, in the time we flew kites, that there was a space in the atmosphere that no kite ever flew in before and that our kite might enter? The sense of boundless possibility should belong to things in stories told to children. This delight in things, this sense of the uniqueness of things, is in every story that children delight in. An old lamp may be Aladdin's. A key may open the door to mystery. A dish may be the supreme possession of a king. For children feel, as people with few possessions feel, the adventure and the enchantment that are in things.

For Educators

There are public occasions on which elders make addresses to young people, telling them that they are about to go into the world. The world that they are thinking of on those occasions is the world of business, of social relations, of mature interests. Beside it, or over against it, there is another world—the world that is within each of the young people whom the address is being made to—the world of thought, meditation, intuition, imagina-

tion. The world of business, of social relationships, mature interests, impresses boys and girls of a certain age, and it is not difficult to prepare them to live in it. And it should not be difficult to show them, not so much how to enter into, but how to keep native in the other world, the world of thought, meditation, intuition, imagination.

To say the least, it is well to have in a growing human being something that responds to the gathering of the clouds before nightfall; to have a feeling about the magnificent lines of an ocean-going ship; to be able to cherish this or that poem; to be able to read history intelligently and to relate it to the events of one's own time; to keep one's mind clear from the passions that take hold of crowds; to be able to communicate with the great people of the age, men and women, should one ever come near them actually. And the growing human being who is being addressed on these occasions would lose the power to feel, or to be able to do such things, if his or her mind is set too exclusively on the world of practical affairs, social relationships, mature interests.

There are no rules for getting on in the world that is alongside or over against our practical world; that world is in ourselves, and we can only get on in it by individual impulse, individual seeking, individual enlightenment. A little can be done to strengthen the impulse, the seeking, the enlightenment. Oral communication of verse and stories is one way. For the human voice, when it can really charge itself with what is in a poem or a story, more powerfully than any other agency, can put into our deeper consciousness those lasting patterns which belong to the deeper consciousness of the race.

Through the possession of a part of the heritage of poetry, of story, children can enter or keep in the world that has been spoken about—the world of imagination, thought, and intuition. It would be well if they could receive some of this heritage orally, and, in the case of poetry, if they could receive it from some one who had regard for the rhythm of the verse, and was able to impart a delight in the rhythm and in the structure of verse. The possession of poetry is a possession that lasts, a possession that no one can take away from whoever has it; it is a talisman that gives an entrance into the world that we may not be separated from without loss to our humanity. For without some ability for making ourselves at home in the world of thought, imagination, intuition, a boy or a girl will never be able to understand all that is summed up in art and philosophy, will never have any deep feeling for religion, and will not be able to get anything out of the reading of history; in short, unless they are somewhat at home in that world, they will live without any fineness in their lives.

Some time, perhaps soon, it will come to be recognized that it is as important to cultivate the imagination as it is to cultivate the will or the intelligence. At present systems of education are directed toward training the will or the intelligence. Perhaps the time is at hand when we will have an education that will be directed toward training the intelligence and the will through the imagination. For imagination is one of the great faculties; it is the one faculty common to all exceptional people—to soldiers, statesmen, saints; to artists, scientists, philosophers, and great business men. Says the Serpent to Eve in "Back to Methuselah," "She told it to me as a marvelous story of something that never happened to a Lillith that never was. She did not know that imagination is the beginning of creation. You imagine what you desire; you will what you imagine; and at last you create what you will." The day may come when that sentence will be written above all places of education: "Imagination is the beginning of creation. You imagine what you desire; you will what you imagine; and at last you create what you will."